BOUND BY LAW?

TALES FROM THE PUBLIC DOMAIN

KEITH AOKI ☆ JAMES BOYLE ☆ JENNIFER JENKINS

Foreword by **DAVIS GUGGENHEIM**

Introduction by **CORY DOCTOROW**

Duke University Press 2008

Duke University Press Cataloging-in-Publication Data
Aoki, Keith
Bound by law? : tales from the public domain / Keith Aoki, James Boyle, and Jennifer Jenkins
—New expanded ed.
    p. cm.—
ISBN 978-0-8223-4371-4 (pbk. : alk. paper)
1. Fair use (Copyright)—United States—Caricatures and cartoons. 2. Public domain (Copyright law)—United States—Caricatures and cartoons. 3. Copyright—United States—Caricatures and cartoons. I. Boyle, James, 1959-. II. Jenkins, Jennifer.
KF3050 .A54 2008   346.730482—dc22

Foreword
by Davis Guggenheim, Academy Award-winning director
of the documentary "An Inconvenient Truth"

As a director and producer of both commercial and non-commercial projects, I find myself on both sides of the war that rages around copyright and the public domain. In my last movie, "An Inconvenient Truth," we had a terrible time clearing footage of all kinds. Simply finding the source and status of archival footage nearly brought my production to its knees. We faced stressful and urgent questions like: Who owns this? Will anyone who thinks they own this sue me? Even though it was considered public domain ten years ago, is there a possibility someone might claim this? Will the lawyers for the production company and studio accept the conclusion I have carefully drawn and allow me to use it in the film? I have lost many shots and sequences because I wasn't able to answer these questions.

The worst example of this happened when I was making a film called "The First Year," a documentary which followed five teachers through their treacherous first year of teaching public school. In the climactic scene, one of the teachers, who is taking his kids on a field trip for the first time, hears the song "Stairway to Heaven" by Led Zeppelin. It is both funny and tragic when he announces to his kids, "This is the greatest song ever written," as he cranks the volume in his rental van. He is possessed with joy, expressing himself for the first time to his students. They are simply bored. Everything in the movie leads up to this moment and when audiences see this scene, they laugh and cry at the same time because it is touching and tragic. But most audiences don't get to see this scene in the film. On the DVD, which is still for sale, that scene has been omitted because I have not been able to secure the rights to "Stairway to Heaven." Through archaic loopholes I could use the song in festival screenings and on PBS, but when it came to any commercial use I was forbidden to use it. Not because I couldn't afford to license the song, but because I could never find the rights holders or their representatives (of which there are many, which is another sad story).

Ten years ago, I would have used the song, citing fair use. Now lawyers for distributors are scared about the chance, just the chance, of a claim against the movie. The problems are twofold. The first is the diminishing world of fair use as the mainstream legal world interprets it. In real terms this means that now when I lift my camera and look through the lens, there is less and less that is free to use: do I have to clear that soda can, that poster, that car or that highrise? What happens to our culture when some of us can pay and others can't?

The other disturbing thing is the uncertainty of it all. Even most legal experts who work on the issue have to roll the dice trying to interpret where the current line of fair use is drawn. You can feel the handwringing when we propose even the most rock solid interpretation to an errors and omissions lawyer. The truth is that most of us just don't know. And that not knowing means that the most stringent interpretation wins. No responsible lawyer wants to expose his client to the possibility of a lawsuit, even if it's only an outside chance.

And so, wonderful moments of magic are cut from movies—simple ones and profound ones. But this doesn't have to happen. Creative Commons helps artists who want to protect their work and to clearly define the way in which their work can be shared. And this wonderful, funny and clever comic makes a very complex issue simple for people like me to understand. I keep a copy in my desk, for when I get confused.

Introduction

by Cory Doctorow, award-winning science fiction author
and co-editor of the blog Boing Boing

Who owns photons? When your camera opens its aperture and greedily gobbles all the light reflecting off the surfaces of buildings, faces, t-shirts, paintings, sculptures, movies, and photos, are you breaking the law? Does your camera's mic infringe when it captures the perturbations made by speech, song and soundtrack?

If these seem like silly questions, blame the law, not the questions. Copyright, a system that is meant to promote creativity, has been hijacked by a few industrial players and perverted. Today, copyright is as likely to suppress new creativity as it is to protect it.

Documentary filmmakers have it tough. The job of a good documentary is to *document*: to set down on video the world as it exists, to tell the story of the world, to lay bare its bones and its deeds.

With every passing year, documenting the world gets more fraught.

Everyone, it seems, has his hand out, asking for a license to merely recount the truth: this billboard stands over that city, this logo appears on that man's t-shirt, this TV program was playing when this event took place.

Some of them don't just want you to take a license. Some of them don't want you to report on them at all.

What's a filmmaker to do?

_____

Before copyright, there was patronage. You were allowed to make art if the Pope or some duke could be convinced that you had a good idea. This generated some lovely ceilings and frescos, but it wasn't exactly democratic.

Copyright industrialized the practice. Now art could be made if an artist could convince a wealthy industrialist that the exclusive right to market the work was worth funding its production. This radically decentralized the decision-making process for art: there are lots more industrialists than Popes, after all.

Today, the industrialists have reinvented themselves as Popes and dukes and kings. If you're signed to a big label—if you have the patronage of a king—that label will clear your way to using samples from the other labels' catalogs in your songs. If you're an indie, forget about it.

If you're a filmmaker working for a big studio, you've got rabid packs of attack-lawyers at your disposal, employed to go forth and negotiate your licenses when you need them. Or even when you don't need them: if you're a studio lawyer, it makes sense to act as though even the most casual or attenuated reproduction requires a license—that way, people will pay you for licenses to your employer's works, too.

If you're an indie, this leaves you out in the cold. You're not on the inside, you don't have white-shoe attorneys standing by to negotiate your "use" of the logo on the shirt of a guy caught on video in a riot.

This isn't how copyright is supposed to work.

———————————

This isn't how copyright works. If you've got lawyers on your side and you're willing to fight, you're likely to find that most of the uses that someone wants you to pay for are in fact permitted without payment or permission, under the doctrine of "Fair Use." But chances are, if you can't afford a license, you can't afford the lawyer to prove that you don't need to pay for the license.

And yet, at this moment, the cost of raw materials of documentary making are in free-fall. Last year's editing suites are being replaced by this year's laptops—the $1500 laptop I'm typing this on has more RAM, processor and hard-drive than the $100,000 Avid suite I used to babysit at a documentary film-house. Democracy Player and Dabble, YouTube and Google Video, the Internet Archive and Dijjer are the leading edge of a movement to make sharing video free and easy. Our pockets bulge with devices that let us watch low-resolution, short videos wherever we are—the perfect small screen for the indie documentary.

Copyright law might work well when it's practiced by corporate attorneys from Fortune 100 companies, but once it impinges on the normal activity of creative people documenting their world, it creates more problems than it solves.

This is a sensible book about a ridiculous subject. It's an example of the principle it illustrates: that taking from the culture around us to make new things is what culture is all about, it's what culture is for. Culture is that which we use to communicate.

The comic form makes this issue into something less abstract, more concrete, and the Duke Public Domain folks who produced this have not just written a treatise on copyright, they've produced a loving tribute to the form of comics.

It's a book whose time has come. Read it, share it. Get angry. Do something. Document your world.

EACH EPISODE IN OUR LITTLE SERIES ABOUT THE ARTS WILL EXAMINE ONE PORTION OF A LEGAL BOUNDARY, A KIND OF **TWILIGHT ZONE.** THIS IS THE LINE BETWEEN **INTELLECTUAL PROPERTY** AND THE **PUBLIC DOMAIN,** THE MYSTERIOUS REALM WHERE MATERIAL IS FREE FOR ALL TO USE WITHOUT PERMISSION.

OUR GUIDES, TWO OBSCURE FIGURES WHO DWELL IN THESE SHADOWS... WHOSE LIVES ARE SPENT IN AN OBSESSIVE QUEST TO CHART THIS LINE, ALMOST AS IF THEY WERE CONDEMNED BY SOME GHASTLY CURSE TO BE THE MAPMAKERS OF **LIMBO.**

CREAK

REVEAL YOURSELVES PLEASE!!

CREAK

CLICK CLACK

CLICK CLACK

CLICK CLACK

CLICK! HI.

HI.

2

AND WHICH OF THESE ARTS SHALL WE DISCUSS TONIGHT?

WILL IT BE MUSIC?

OR ANIMATION?

WILL IT BE COMIC BOOKS?

Pink Pearl

NO...

TONIGHT WE ARE LOOKING AT THE PLACE WHERE ART MEETS HISTORY, WHERE REPORTING MEETS THE FEATURE FILM...

TONIGHT WE ARE LOOKING AT... DOCUMENTARY FILM...

HEH HEH HEH

A YOUNG PERSON'S GUIDE TO INTELLECTUAL PROPERTY AND DOCUMENTARY FILMMAKING

CRUMB

SHOAH

STOP MAKING SENSE

HOOP DREAMS

Harlan County USA

ACADEMY AWARD WINNER!

A FILM BY SPIKE LEE

4 Little Girls

WOODSTOCK

Depeche Mode 101

Wh The Kids Are Alright

SO, TO BEGIN...

DOCUMENTARIES ARE RECORDS OF OUR CULTURE. BUT OUR CULTURE IS FULL OF ARTIFACTS PROTECTED BY INTELLECTUAL PROPERTY RIGHTS -- MUSIC, IMAGES, PHOTOGRAPHS.

FILMMAKERS ARE SOMETIMES ASKED TO CLEAR RIGHTS TO THESE CULTURAL FRAGMENTS, EVEN IF THEY APPEAR ONLY INCIDENTALLY.

"CLEARING RIGHTS" IS THE PROCESS OF FINDING THE RIGHTS HOLDER, AND GETTING PERMISSION OR PAYING TO USE MATERIAL.

BUT DOCUMENTARIANS ARE NOT MERELY IN THE POSITION OF DEALING WITH OTHER PEOPLE'S RIGHTS, THEY'RE ALSO IN THE POSITION OF ASSERTING THEIR OWN -- THEY MAY WANT TO RECEIVE PAYMENT, OR PREVENT CERTAIN USES OF THEIR FOOTAGE.

HOW SHOULD THE LAW DRAW LINES BETWEEN FILMMAKERS' NEED TO PORTRAY A CULTURE FULL OF LEGALLY PROTECTED MATERIAL, AND THEIR DESIRE TO PROTECT THEIR OWN WORKS?

LET'S HEAR FROM A FILMMAKER

MEET AKIKO...

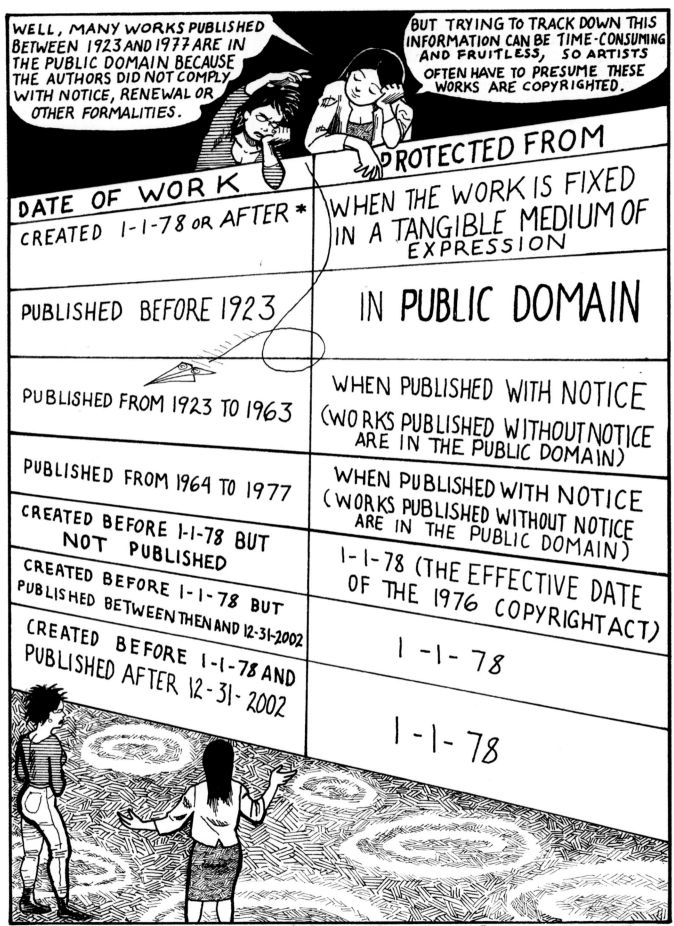

WELL, MANY WORKS PUBLISHED BETWEEN 1923 AND 1977 ARE IN THE PUBLIC DOMAIN BECAUSE THE AUTHORS DID NOT COMPLY WITH NOTICE, RENEWAL OR OTHER FORMALITIES.

BUT TRYING TO TRACK DOWN THIS INFORMATION CAN BE TIME-CONSUMING AND FRUITLESS, SO ARTISTS OFTEN HAVE TO PRESUME THESE WORKS ARE COPYRIGHTED.

DATE OF WORK	PROTECTED FROM
CREATED 1-1-78 OR AFTER *	WHEN THE WORK IS FIXED IN A TANGIBLE MEDIUM OF EXPRESSION
PUBLISHED BEFORE 1923	IN PUBLIC DOMAIN
PUBLISHED FROM 1923 TO 1963	WHEN PUBLISHED WITH NOTICE (WORKS PUBLISHED WITHOUT NOTICE ARE IN THE PUBLIC DOMAIN)
PUBLISHED FROM 1964 TO 1977	WHEN PUBLISHED WITH NOTICE (WORKS PUBLISHED WITHOUT NOTICE ARE IN THE PUBLIC DOMAIN)
CREATED BEFORE 1-1-78 BUT NOT PUBLISHED	1-1-78 (THE EFFECTIVE DATE OF THE 1976 COPYRIGHT ACT)
CREATED BEFORE 1-1-78 BUT PUBLISHED BETWEEN THEN AND 12-31-2002	1-1-78
CREATED BEFORE 1-1-78 AND PUBLISHED AFTER 12-31-2002	1-1-78

*WORKS PUBLISHED WITHOUT NOTICE BETWEEN 1-1-78 AND 3-1-89 RETAINED COPYRIGHT ONLY IF THE OMISSION OF NOTICE WAS CORRECTED.

TERM OF PROTECTION	EXAMPLE
LIFE OF AUTHOR + 70 YEARS (FOR WORKS OF CORPORATE OR ANONYMOUS AUTHORSHIP THE SHORTER OF 95 YEARS FROM PUBLICATION OR 120 YEARS FROM CREATION)	HEH HEH / METALLICA
NONE	MOBY DICK HERMAN MELVILLE
95 YEARS AFTER PUBLICATION DATE; HOWEVER IF COPYRIGHT WAS NOT RENEWED, WORK IS NOW IN PUBLIC DOMAIN	GONE WITH THE WIND
95 YEARS AFTER PUBLICATION DATE	Fear AND LOATHING
LIFE + 70 YEARS	INK / Dear Diary, Today I went to my Property Law Class / and you know that I don't like Law
LIFE + 70 YEARS, OR 12-31-2047, WHICHEVER IS GREATER	NEVER BEFORE PUBLISHED! THE LETTERS OF MARK TWAIN
LIFE + 70 YEARS	K-TEL 2005 GREAT UNRELEASED GARAGE BANDS FROM THE 1960s

* BASED ON PROFESSOR LOLLY GASAWAY'S CHART "WHEN U.S. WORKS PASS INTO THE PUBLIC DOMAIN."

FAIR USE *SHOULD* MEAN YOU DON'T NEED PERMISSION FOR INCIDENTALLY CAPTURED FRAGMENTS. BUT THE PRACTICE IS OFTEN DIFFERENT.

JON ELSE'S EXPERIENCE IS **NOT** UNIQUE.

MAD HOT *Ballroom*

A CELL PHONE HAPPENED TO RING DURING THE FILMING OF MARILYN AGRELO AND AMY SEWELL'S "MAD HOT BALLROOM," A DOCUMENTARY ABOUT NEW YORK CITY KIDS IN A BALLROOM DANCING COMPETITION. THE RING TONE WAS THE "ROCKY" THEME SONG. THIS IS A VERY STRONG CASE FOR FAIR USE.

DA DA DA DA DA DA DA DA DA DA DUH DA DA DUH

BUT EMI, WHICH OWNS THE RIGHTS TO THE "ROCKY" SONG, ASKED FOR -- GUESS HOW MUCH?

$10,000!

I DUNNO... HOW MUCH?

IN ANOTHER SCENE, THEY WERE FILMING A FOOSBALL GAME AND ONE OF THE PLAYERS SPONTANEOUSLY YELLED "EVERYBODY DANCE NOW," A LINE FROM THE C & C MUSIC FACTORY HIT.

WARNER CHAPPELL DEMANDED $5000 FOR USE OF THE LINE.

THEY EVENTUALLY GOT A BETTER DEAL ON THE "ROCKY" RING TONE, BUT DECIDED TO CUT THE "DANCE" LINE, EVEN THOUGH IT REALLY FIT THE MOVIE'S THEME.

IN "THE FIRST YEAR," A PBS DOCUMENTARY ABOUT LOS ANGELES PUBLIC SCHOOL TEACHERS IN THEIR FIRST YEAR OF TEACHING, LED ZEPPELIN'S "STAIRWAY TO HEAVEN" CAME ON THE RADIO WHILE A TEACHER WAS DRIVING A VAN FULL OF STUDENTS TO AN OUTING.

THE TEACHER TURNED THE SONG UP AND CALLED TO THE CLASS TO LISTEN. THE STUDENTS ROLLED THEIR EYES. IT WASN'T THEIR MUSIC. IT WAS A PIVOTAL MOMENT-- A LIVE GENERATION GAP.

DAVIS GUGGENHEIM, THE FILMMAKER, WAS UNABLE TO CLEAR RIGHTS TO THE SONG AND HAD TO CUT IT OUT...

WOW, THAT'S DEMORALIZING. THERE'S A LOT OF MUSIC PLAYING IN THE BACKGROUND OF MY FILM. I DIDN'T CHOOSE TO INCLUDE IT. IT WAS JUST THERE, EVERYWHERE I FILMED.

WHAT ARE MY OPTIONS?

WELL, YOU COULD ASSERT FAIR USE AND KEEP IT IN THE FILM...

OR TRY TO FIND THE RIGHTS OWNERS AND ASK FOR PERMISSION...

OR OVERDUB IT WITH MUSIC THAT'S IN THE PUBLIC DOMAIN...

HMMM... LET'S SEE...

COULD THE SAX PLAYER IN THE SUBWAY BE PLAYING MOZART INSTEAD OF "I LOVE NEW YORK?"

LEXINGTON AVE

I ♥ NEW YORK

REPLACE THE ROY ORBISON SUNG BY THE STREET MUSICIAN WITH "OH SUSANNAH."

OH PRETTY WOMAN, WALKIN' DOWN THE STREET

AND THE DUELLING HIP HOP SONGS IN TIMES SQUARE WITH JOHN PHILLIP SOUSA...

BOOM THAK

BAM THI

AND REPLACE THE HOT DOG VENDOR'S SINATRA WITH "YES! WE HAVE NO BANANAS."

SABRETT FRANKFURTERS ICE COLD DRINKS

COURT

I DID IT MY WAY!!

AKIKO... UM... THAT SONG WAS SET TO GO INTO THE PUBLIC DOMAIN IN 1999, BUT THEN CONGRESS EXTENDED THE TERM FOR ANOTHER 20 YEARS...

?

THE THING IS, THE MUSIC IS AN IMPORTANT PART OF THESE SCENES, REPLACING IT WOULD REALLY DISRUPT THE FILM.

HMMM...

18

NO, THINGS HAVE CHANGED. AND THE LAW ISN'T NECESSARILY DRIVING THIS. FAIR USE ACTUALLY PROTECTS SOME THINGS MORE CLEARLY TODAY.

BUT MANY FACTORS - NEW TECHNOLOGIES ... NEW MARKETS,... HAVE CONTRIBUTED TO THE RISE OF A "RIGHTS" CULTURE.

BOB DYLAN DONT LOOK BACK
A FILM BY D.A. PENNEBAKER

UNTIL RECENTLY NO ONE INSISTED ON PAYMENT FOR INCIDENTAL USES...

IF YOU WATCH THE END OF "DONT LOOK BACK," D. A. PENNEBAKER'S 1967 DOCUMENTARY ABOUT DYLAN, YOU'LL SEE THAT THERE AREN'T THE TEN MINUTES OF MUSIC CREDITS THAT YOU MIGHT SEE NOW.

WE USED TO ACCEPT THAT COPYRIGHT DIDN'T GIVE CONTROL OVER EVERY USE.

NOW A LOT OF PEOPLE THINK THE RIGHTS ARE ABSOLUTE!

REMEMBER MONTY PYTHON?

SURE. WHY?

IN THE EARLY 70s, TERRY GILLIAM MAY HAVE BORROWED HUNDREDS OF IMAGES FOR HIS MONTY PYTHON ANIMATIONS...

HE DIDN'T HAVE TO GET PERMISSION.

TIMES CHANGE. 20 YEARS LATER, A COURT STOPPED DISTRIBUTION OF HIS MOVIE "12 MONKEYS" ...FINDING THAT GILLIAM HAD BASED A SET DESIGN ON A COPYRIGHTED DRAWING.

REPORTEDLY, HE HAD TO PAY SIX FIGURES TO USE THE SET DESIGN.

12 MONKEYS

WHAT'S IRONIC IS THAT TERRY GILLIAM SUPPOSEDLY ALSO HAD TO PAY FOR A BACKGROUND APPEARANCE OF WARHOL'S **XEROX** OF DA VINCI'S "LAST SUPPER"--ITSELF A COPY OF A PRE-EXISTING WORK!!

THAT **IS** IRONIC!! AND IMAGINE LOSING THOSE MONTY PYTHON COLLAGES!

AND THEN THERE ARE CRITICAL USES...

RELYING ON FAIR USE, ROBERT GREENWALD MADE EXTENSIVE USE OF FOX NEWS CLIPS IN HIS CRITICAL DOCUMENTARY "OUTFOXED."

BOWLING FOR COLUMBINE

MICHAEL MOORE BOWLING FOR COLUMBINE

IN A DISCUSSION OF RACISM IN THE MEDIA, "BOWLING FOR COLUMBINE" USED UNCLEARED FOOTAGE OF NEWS ANCHORS WARNING ABOUT BLACK MALE SUSPECTS.

AND NEITHER USE WAS CHALLENGED!

OUTFOXED:
Rupert Murdoch's War on Journalism

IN FACT, SEVERAL FILMMAKERS' ORGANIZATIONS HAVE JOINTLY PRODUCED A **STATEMENT** of **BEST PRACTICES** in **FAIR USE** TO CLARIFY HOW PROFESSIONAL FILMMAKERS INTERPRET FAIR USE IN DAILY PRACTICE.

FILMMAKERS COULD CHANGE THE "RIGHTS" CULTURE BY LEARNING MORE ABOUT FAIR USE, AND EVEN MAKING SOME COLLECTIVE DECISIONS ABOUT WHAT'S FAIR.

IRONICALLY, ONE REASON LICENSING FEES ARE GOING UP IS THE INCREASING POPULARITY OF DOCUMENTARIES AND NEW MARKETS FOR ARCHIVAL FOOTAGE. THE MAKERS OF PROFITABLE DOCUMENTARIES ABOUT MARILYN MONROE OR THE NORMANDY LANDINGS MIGHT BE ABLE TO AFFORD HIGHER FEES.

BUT THEN WE TRANSFER THIS "PAY AS YOU GO" ATTITUDE TO LESS COMMERCIALLY ATTRACTIVE FILMS ABOUT PUBLIC SCHOOL REFORM OR MENTAL INSTITUTIONS.

SOMETIMES CULTURAL HEROES GET IN ON THE ACTION. THE MARTIN LUTHER KING, JR. ESTATE HAS AGGRESSIVELY ASSERTED COPYRIGHT OVER DR. KING'S SPEECHES, PHOTOS AND INTERVIEWS. THIS CREATED ENORMOUS OBSTACLES FOR DOCUMENTARIES— SUCH AS ORLANDO BAGWELL'S "CITIZEN KING."

ORLANDO BAGWELL

ONE CAN UNDERSTAND WANTING TO PROTECT DR. KING.

BUT ANY RULES THAT APPLY TO MARTIN LUTHER KING WILL ALSO APPLY TO DAVID DUKE.

DO WE WANT TO GIVE COPYRIGHT HOLDERS A **VETO** OVER **HISTORY**?

DISAPPEARING HISTORY, FRIVOLOUS LAWSUITS... THIS SYSTEM DOESN'T MAKE ANY SENSE.

AND YOU KNOW WHAT?

I FEEL LIKE I'M IN A BAD SUPERHERO COMIC...

OUR CULTURE UNDER ASSAULT...

BY A CRAZED OUT-OF-CONTROL "RIGHTS-MONSTER."

FAIR USE

HOW DID WE GET TO THIS STATE OF AFFAIRS? WHAT'S THIS SYSTEM FOR? IS COPYRIGHT ACTUALLY **BAD** FOR ARTISTS?

FOR MORE INFORMATION SEE: http://creativecommons.org/

Creative Commons is a nonprofit that offers a flexible copyright for creative work.

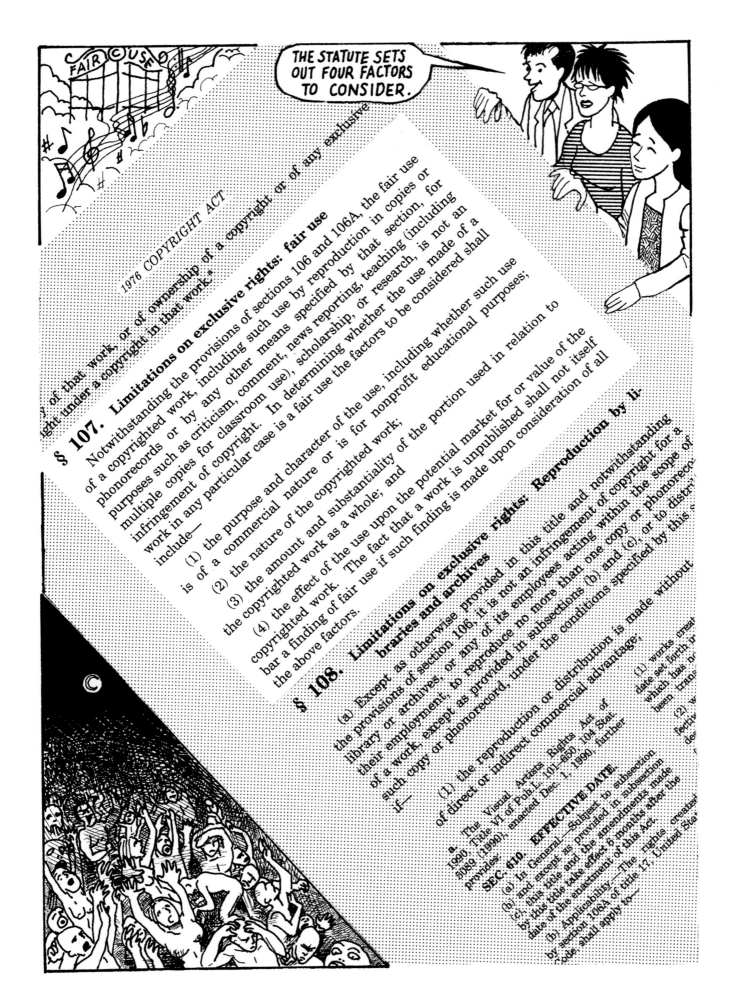

THE STATUTE SETS OUT FOUR FACTORS TO CONSIDER.

FAIR USE

1976 COPYRIGHT ACT

..., of that work, or of ownership of a copyright, or of any exclusive
...ght under a copyright in that work.ª

§ 107. Limitations on exclusive rights: fair use

Notwithstanding the provisions of sections 106 and 106A, the fair use
of a copyrighted work, including such use by reproduction in copies or
phonorecords or by any other means specified by that section, for
purposes such as criticism, comment, news reporting, teaching (including
multiple copies for classroom use), scholarship, or research, is not an
infringement of copyright. In determining whether the use made of a
work in any particular case is a fair use the factors to be considered shall
include—

(1) the purpose and character of the use, including whether such use
is of a commercial nature or is for nonprofit educational purposes;

(2) the nature of the copyrighted work;

(3) the amount and substantiality of the portion used in relation to
the copyrighted work as a whole; and

(4) the effect of the use upon the potential market for or value of the
copyrighted work. The fact that a work is unpublished shall not itself
bar a finding of fair use if such finding is made upon consideration of all
the above factors.

**§ 108. Limitations on exclusive rights: Reproduction by li-
braries and archives**

(a) Except as otherwise provided in this title and notwithstanding
the provisions of section 106, it is not an infringement of copyright for a
library or archives, or any of its employees acting within the scope of
their employment, to reproduce no more than one copy or phonorecord of
a work, except as provided in subsections (b) and (c), or to distri...
such copy or phonorecord, under the conditions specified by this s...
if—

(1) the reproduction or distribution is made without ...
of direct or indirect commercial advantage;

a. The Visual Artists Rights Act of
1990, Title VI of Pub. L. 101–650, 104 Stat.
5089, (1990), enacted Dec. 1, 1990, further
provides,

SEC. 610. EFFECTIVE DATE

(a) In General.—Subject to subsection
(b), and except as provided in subsection
(c), this title and the amendments made
by this title take effect 6 months after the
date of the enactment of this Act.

(b) Applicability.—The rights cre...
by section 106A of title 17, United Sta...
Code shall apply to—

(1) works crea...
date set forth i...
which has n...
been tran...

(2) w...
per...
de...

36

Sony v. Universal Studios (1984)
Fair use: home videotaping of television shows.

"Time-shifting," or videotaping television shows in order to watch them later, was fair use, said the Supreme Court, even though VCR users were copying the entire programs. One key reason was that the time-shifting was private and non-commercial. That meant that the film companies had to prove market harm. The Court did not believe they had done so.

Campbell v. Acuff-Rose (1994)
Fair use: a rap parody of "Pretty Woman".

The rap group 2 Live Crew made a song called "Pretty Woman" that borrowed the bass riff, much of the tune and some lyrics from Roy Orbison's "Oh, Pretty Woman." 2 Live Crew seemed to have 2 strikes against them. They used a lot of the song, and their use was "commercial." The Supreme Court said that even so, this could be fair use. They saw the song as a parody. It "juxtaposes the romantic musings of a man whose fantasy comes true, with degrading taunts, a bawdy demand for sex, and a sigh of relief from paternal responsibility." Because the song was a parody, 2 Live Crew was also allowed to copy more of it – as effective parodies need to "conjure up the original."

Margaret Mitchell

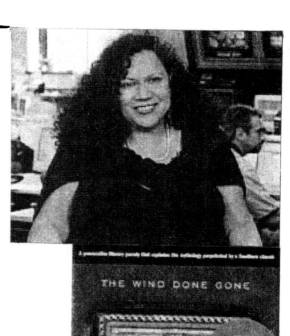

Suntrust v. Houghton Mifflin (2001)
Fair use: a parody of "Gone with the Wind" from a slave's point of view.

Author Alice Randall wrote a parody of *Gone with the Wind* criticizing its romanticized depiction of slavery and the antebellum South, and in doing so alluded to copyrighted characters and scenes from *Gone with the Wind*.

THE WIND DONE GONE

THE UNAUTHORIZED PARODY

ALICE RANDALL

FRANKLY MY DEAR, THEY SHOULDN'T HAVE GIVEN A DAMN!

The Court of Appeals held that this could be fair use: "It is hard to imagine how Randall could have specifically criticized *Gone with the Wind* without depending heavily upon copyrighted elements of that book. A parody is a work that seeks to comment upon or criticize another work by appropriating elements of the original..."

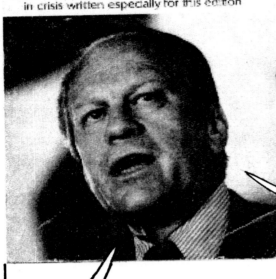

A TIME TO HEAL

With a new introduction about today's America in crisis written especially for this edition

HE'S NOT A CROOK...

...BUT THEY ARE!

The Nation.

Time Magazine agreed to purchase the exclusive right to print a pre-publication excerpt of ex-president Ford's autobiography. Before Time's article came out, the political magazine The Nation got an unauthorized copy of the manuscript. The Nation published its own article, which included 300-400 words from Ford's autobiography about his decision to pardon President Nixon. The Supreme Court said this was not a fair use. Why? The memoirs had not been published yet, and authors have a right to decide whether and when their work will be published. The Court found that The Nation had "effectively arrogated to itself the right of first publication" for the purpose of "scooping" Time's planned article. (Time then canceled the article.) The Court also said that the parts of Ford's book used, though small, were its "heart" – the most powerful and interesting part.

SO HOW DOES ALL THIS APPLY TO ME?

WELL, COURTS HAVE FOUND FAIR USE WHEN DOCUMENTARIES USE SHORT CLIPS IN TRANSFORMATIVE — NEW, DIFFERENT AND VALUABLE — WAYS, INSTEAD OF MERELY "RIPPING OFF" THE COPYRIGHTED MATERIAL.

HERE'S SOME EXAMPLES OF USES THAT WERE FOUND TO BE "FAIR."

ORIGINAL MOTION PICTURE SOUNDTRACKS

INVASION OF THE SAUCER-MEN

IT CONQUERED THE WORLD

MUSIC COMPOSED AND CONDUCTED BY RONALD STEIN

The documentary *Aliens Invade Hollywood* could use 3 clips totaling 48 seconds (1%) from *Invasion of the Saucermen* to show early film portrayals of alien visitations and government cover-ups.

THIS IS A FAIR USE — SO LONG AS YOU DON'T MENTION AREA 51!!!!

DON'T WORRY MA'AM, THAT EXCERPT DIDN'T SHOW A REAL UFO... SWAMP GAS FROM A WEATHER BALLOON...,

An A&E biography of Peter Graves could use 20 seconds (less than 1%) of *It Conquered the World*, which starred Graves, to show his modest beginnings in the film business.

THIS MOVIE, SHOULD YOU CHOOSE TO EXCERPT IT, WILL SELF-DESTRUCT IN 20 SECONDS!

A TBS biography of Muhammad Ali could use 9-14 clips totaling between 41 seconds and 2 minutes (between .7 and 2.1%) from *When We Were Kings*, a documentary focusing on the "Rumble in the Jungle" fight in Zaire between Ali and George Foreman. (The parties disagreed about the number of clips, so the court used the 9-14 range.)

AN THAT LADEEZ `N GENTZ—IS A... FAIR USE !!!

IN ALL THESE CASES, THE COURTS THOUGHT THE USES WERE "TRANSFORMATIVE" BECAUSE THE PURPOSE OF THE ORIGINAL MOVIES WAS TO ENTERTAIN VIEWERS, WHILE THE DOCUMENTARIES USED THE CLIPS FOR COMMENTARY AND CRITICISM.

FAIR USE MEANS YOU CAN QUOTE LIKE A BUTTERFLY, STING LIKE A BEE !!

ALSO, THE CLIPS WEREN'T "THE HEART" OF THE MOVIES THEY WERE TAKEN FROM AND WERE "TOO FEW, TOO SHORT, AND TOO SMALL IN RELATION TO THE WHOLE" TO UNDERCUT THE MARKET FOR THOSE FILMS.

The Definitive Elvis, a 16-hour documentary that advertised its "all-encompassing" collection of Elvis appearances, used clips from *The Ed Sullivan Show*, *The Steve Allen Show*, and Elvis TV specials. The court thought that these uses went beyond biographical reference and were just rebroadcast as entertainment, often without commentary or interruption. Even though the clips were short – ranging from a few seconds to a minute, many were "the heart" of the original shows, including the moments when Elvis sang his most famous songs.

EVEN IN FEATURE FILMS, THE USE OF TRADE MARKS TO DEPICT "REALITY" HAS BEEN PROTECTED BY COURTS.

CATERPILLAR SUED DISNEY CLAIMING THAT "GEORGE OF THE JUNGLE 2" INFRINGED ITS TRADEMARKS.

IN THE FILM, THE EVIL INDUSTRIALIST TRIES TO DESTROY GEORGE'S JUNGLE WITH "CATERPILLAR" BULLDOZERS. A FEDERAL COURT REFUSED TO BLOCK THE FILM'S RELEASE.

HA! HA! HAHA!!

THE COURT SAID:

"THE APPEARANCE OF PRODUCTS BEARING WELL KNOWN TRADEMARKS IN CINEMA AND TELEVISION IS A COMMON PHENOMENON."

WHAT ABOUT GETTING PERMISSION FROM PEOPLE WHO APPEAR IN THE DOCUMENTARY?

PERMISSION IS NORMALLY REQUIRED -- PRIVACY IS A LEGITIMATE CLAIM.

WHAZZUP?

BUT THERE IS AN IMPORTANT FIRST AMENDMENT EXCEPTION THAT LETS YOU SHOW PEOPLE INVOLVED IN MATTERS OF PUBLIC INTEREST, WITHOUT PERMISSION.

CONSIDER FILMMAKER MICHAEL MOORE...

MICHAEL MOORE INTERVIEWED JAMES NICHOLS, BROTHER OF TERRY NICHOLS, IN THE DOCUMENTARY "BOWLING FOR COLUMBINE." MOORE SUGGESTED THAT NICHOLS MIGHT HAVE SOME CONNECTION TO THE OKLAHOMA CITY BOMBING ("The Feds didn't have the goods on James, so the charges were dropped.") NICHOLS SUED, CLAIMING MOORE HAD DEFAMED HIM, BUT HE ALSO SAID THAT HIS "RIGHT OF PUBLICITY" HAD BEEN VIOLATED. THE COURT HELD THAT BECAUSE THE FILM ADDRESSED A MATTER OF IMPORTANT PUBLIC CONCERN -- VIOLENCE IN AMERICA -- AND NICHOLS WAS PART OF THE BOMBING STORY, MOORE'S USE OF NICHOLS WAS SPEECH PROTECTED BY THE FIRST AMENDMENT.

DUDE, WHERE'S MY LAWSUIT?

EVEN WHEN THE DOCUMENTARY ISN'T ABOUT SUCH CONTROVERSIAL ISSUES, SOME STATE LAWS ALLOW THE FILMMAKER TO USE A PERSON'S PICTURE WITHOUT PERMISSION IF THE SUBJECT IS "NEWS" OR "PUBLIC AFFAIRS." AND "PUBLIC AFFAIRS" CAN BE DEFINED PRETTY BROADLY.

A DOCUMENTARY ABOUT THE EARLY DAYS OF MALIBU USED SOME FOOTAGE OF FAMOUS SURFER MICKEY DORA, WHO SUED FOR UNAUTHORIZED USE OF HIS IMAGE.

THE CALIFORNIA LAW HAD AN EXCEPTION FOR PUBLIC AFFAIRS AND THE JUDGE SAID A SURFING DOCUMENTARY QUALIFIED.

"[SURFING] HAS CREATED A LIFESTYLE THAT INFLUENCES SPEECH, BEHAVIOR, DRESS, AND ENTERTAINMENT, AMONG OTHER THINGS."

TO SAY NOTHING ABOUT CREATING AN INTERGALACTIC SUPERHERO!!

51

SO, AS LONG AS I UNDERSTAND THE LIMITS OF THE LAW, I'M SET, RIGHT?

YOU'VE HEARD OF ERRORS AND OMISSIONS INSURANCE?

YES, E & O INSURANCE.

WELL, REGARDLESS OF WHAT THE LAW SAYS, RIGHTS CLEARANCES MAY PLAY OUT DIFFERENTLY IN PRACTICE...

HBO

TO SHOW YOUR FILM TO A BROADER PUBLIC THROUGH CONVENTIONAL DISTRIBUTION CHANNELS - LIKE HBO OR PBS - YOU NEED E & O INSURANCE TO COVER POSSIBLE LAWSUITS.

INSURANCE COMPANIES, UNDERSTANDABLY RISK AVERSE, TYPICALLY REQUIRE A DETAILED LIST OF THE SOURCE AND LICENSING STATUS OF THE MATERIAL IN THE FILM...

SO, WHAT I CAN AND CANNOT USE DEPENDS ON WHAT THE BROADCASTER, DISTRIBUTOR, INSURANCE COMPANY, BROKERS AND LAWYERS ARE COMFORTABLE WITH?

AND BECAUSE THEY GENERALLY DON'T ACKNOWLEDGE "FAIR USE" CLAIMS, THEY MAY REQUIRE CLEARANCES WELL BEYOND THOSE REQUIRED BY THE LAW.

FAIR USES MAY HAVE TO BE CLEARED BY AN ARMY OF LAWYERS OR CUT FROM THE FILM?

...BUT I WOULDN'T EXPECT PAYMENT IF MY DOCUMENTARY WAS PLAYING IN THE BACKGROUND OF ANOTHER SHOT!

IF THE GOAL OF COPYRIGHT IS TO ENCOURAGE PEOPLE TO CREATE, THEN THESE KINDS OF RIGHTS CLEARANCES DON'T MAKE ANY SENSE...

IS ANYONE BETTER OFF WITH ALL THESE PAYMENTS FOR TINY FRAGMENTS OF CULTURE?

IS THE IDEA THAT ARTISTS WON'T MAKE FILMS OR MUSIC, UNLESS THEY HAVE THE RIGHT TO CONTROL A FEW SECONDS IN A DOCUMENTARY?

56

ALL OF THIS INFORMATION HAS BEEN REALLY USEFUL. WHEN I'M DEALING WITH RIGHTS CLEARANCE ISSUES, I'LL HAVE A MUCH BETTER IDEA OF WHAT'S GOING ON.

AND WE'VE ONLY BEEN DISCUSSING WHAT THE LAW AND PRACTICES CURRENTLY ARE --- **ONE** REASON THEY'RE THIS WAY IS BECAUSE PEOPLE ASSUME THAT'S WHAT ARTISTS WANT. BUT THE LAW AND THE "RIGHTS" CULTURE **CAN** CHANGE IF ENOUGH ARTISTS ARE UNHAPPY WITH THEM!

WHATEVER HAPPENS YOU'VE CONVINCED ME OF THIS, I'M NOT GOING TO PRODUCE AN AIRBRUSHED OR FICTIONALIZED VERSION OF THIS DOCUMENTARY!

BUT WHAT ABOUT THE BIGGER ISSUE?

WHAT KIND OF COPYRIGHT SYSTEM DO WE WANT?

THESE SHADOWS HAVE DANCED FOR YOU FOR A FRAGMENT OF TIME.

PERHAPS SOMETHING IN THEIR WORDS HAS CAUGHT YOUR ATTENTION, TAUGHT YOU SOMETHING, GIVEN YOU AN IDEA?

A YOUNG PERSON'S GUIDE TO INTELLECTUAL PROPER...

BUT NOW THEIR MOMENT IN THE LIGHT IS OVER.

UNTIL THE NEXT TIME WE MEET, ALL THAT IS LEFT IS...

NOT YET...

WAIT...

SILENCE.

Afterword
The True Story of *Bound By Law.*
(or 'Why Three Stodgy Academics Wrote a Comic Book')
James Boyle

The authors of this book are frequent, and for the most part, appreciative users of the law of copyright. Keith trained as an artist, has published several comic books and many scholarly articles, and is the bass player for The Garden Weasels – a band that is generally described as being "pretty good considering it is made up entirely of law professors." Apart from her academic work, Jennifer is also a pianist, filmmaker and short story writer. James has written books and numerous articles, and is a columnist for the *Financial Times* online. He also serves on the Board of Creative Commons, a non-profit organization that provides simplified copyright tools for artists and creators. We have all authored copyrighted works, cashed royalty checks, and benefitted from the ability to make "fair use" of copyrighted material in our own creations, whether artistic or scholarly. And we are all also scholars and teachers of copyright law – studying its history, its goals, its constitutional basis, and its impact on the arts. In the process, we have come to admire the way that copyright law has adapted to new media and new technologies through history, maintaining its balance between the realm of ownership and the realm of the public domain – where material is free for all to use without permission or fee. So count us as stodgy believers in the copyright system, not revolutionaries eager to scrap the whole thing.

But from the depths of our stodginess comes this little message – the system appears to have gone astray, to have lost sight of its original goal. Does anyone believe that "the progress of science and the useful arts" is furthered by requiring documentary filmmakers to clear every fragment of copyrighted material caught in their films – even a copyrighted ring-tone on a phone, or a fleeting fragment of TV in the background of a shot? To be fair, in many – perhaps most – cases these demands for payment or clearance have nothing to do with copyright law as it stands. Instead, they are a

manifestation of a "permissions culture" premised on the belief that copyright gives its owners the right to demand payment for *every* type of usage, no matter its length, or its purpose, or the context in which it is set. But that is not, and never has been the law. Copyright may also be adjusting poorly to a world in which everyone can have their own digital printing press; the citizen publishers of cyberspace, the young digital artists, filmmakers and musicians, are unlikely to have high-priced lawyers advising them. The flourishing of digital media has been seen by policymakers mainly as a threat

– as the rise of a "pirate culture of lawlessness." That threat is real. But what is missing is a sense of the corresponding opportunity.

Copyright is not an end in itself. It is a tool to promote the creation and distribution of knowledge and culture. What could be a better manifestation of this goal than a world in which there are few barriers to entry, where a blog can break a major political scandal, a $218 digital film can go to the Cannes Film Festival, a podcast can reach tens of thousands of listeners, a mash-up can savagely criticize the government's response to a hurricane, where recording and remixing technology better than anything Phil Spector ever had may come bundled free with your laptop? Yet for many of these new digital creators, copyright appears more as an obstacle than as an aid. Sometimes – as with many of the examples we described in this comic book – that may be the result of simple misinformation, a culture of fear and legal threats, or private gatekeepers using copyright law as an excuse to impose deals on artists who lack the information and power to protest. At other times, it seems the law genuinely has lost its internal balance and needs to be reformed – one example might be the extraordinary retrospective lengthening of the copyright term. Just as the digital revolution allows us to offer cheap access to the texts, movies, music and images of the twentieth century, we have extended the length of copyright terms so that most of those cultural artifacts are off limits, even though they are commercially unavailable and their authors cannot be found. But if copyright has sometimes failed, or been applied so that it fails, the answer is not to ignore it, to lose respect for it, to violate it.

One of the under-appreciated tragedies of the permissions culture is that many young artists only experience copyright as an impediment, a source of incomprehensible demands for payment, cease and desist letters, and legal transaction costs. Technology allows them to mix, to combine, to create collages. They see law as merely an obstacle. This is a shame because copyright can be a valuable tool for artists and creators of all kinds - even for many of those who are trying to share their work without charge. Copyright can work in the culture of mash-ups, parodies and remixes, of hypertext links and online educational materials. But it can do so only if we do not let the system slide further out of balance.

We thought about how to present these messages to an audience of artists and filmmakers, how to pass on the information that they need to make the system work for them. But at the same time we wanted to reach a wider audience – an audience of citizens and policymakers who generally hear nothing about copyright except the drumbeat of "Piracy! Piracy! Piracy!" The story of documentary film is vitally important in its own right. Documentaries are the most vivid visual record of our history, our controversies and our culture. But their story is also a manifestation of a wider problem and one that we thought could enrich the public debate on the subject.

For some strange reason, none of our intended audiences seem eager to read scholarly law review articles. What's more, there is something perverse about explaining an essentially visual and frequently surreal reality in gray, lawyerly prose. Finally, what could better illustrate the process we describe than a work which has to feature literally hundreds of copyrighted works in order to tell its story, a living exercise in fair use? Hence this book. It is the first in a series from Duke's Center for the Study of the Public Domain dealing with the effects of intellectual property on art and culture. We hope you enjoy it. For those who are interested in the wider debate on the ownership and control of science and knowledge, or the ideas behind "cultural environmentalism," links to other resources are given on the next page.

Center for the Study of the Public Domain
Duke Law School http://www.law.duke.edu/cspd

"The mission of the Center is to promote research and scholarship on the contributions of the public domain to speech, culture, science and innovation, to promote debate about the balance needed in our intellectual property system and to translate academic research into public policy solutions." An online version of this work is available for free at our website.

Further Reading on Intellectual Property and Culture
James Boyle, The Second Enclosure Movement & the Construction of the Public Domain
http://www.law.duke.edu/pd/papers/boyle.pdf
"It may sound paradoxical, but in a very real sense protection of the commons was one of the fundamental goals of intellectual property law. In the new vision of intellectual property, however, property should be extended everywhere - more is better. Expanding patentable and copyrightable subject matter, lengthening the copyright term, giving legal protection to 'digital barbed wire' even if it is used in part to protect against fair use: Each of these can be understood as a vote of no-confidence in the productive powers of the commons...."

Collected Papers on the Public Domain (Duke: L&CP 2003)
http://www.law.duke.edu/journals/lcp/indexpd.htm
"What does the public domain do? What is its importance, its history, its role in science, art, and in the building of the Internet? How is the public domain similar to and different from the idea of a commons? Is it constitutionally protected, or required by the norms of free expression? This edited collection, the first to focus on the public domain, seeks to answer those questions. Its topics range across a broad swath of innovation and creativity, from science and the Internet to music and culture jamming. Its list of authors includes prominent environmental scholars, appropriation artists, legal theorists, historians and literary critics."

Lawrence Lessig, Free Culture (The Penguin Press, New York 2004)
"A technology has given us a new freedom. Slowly, some begin to understand that this freedom need not mean anarchy. We can carry a free culture into the twenty-first century, without artists losing and without the potential of digital technology being destroyed.... Common sense must revolt. It must act to free culture. Soon, if this potential is ever to be realized."

A Sampling of Legal Resources: These are not a substitute for legal advice. For specific legal questions please consult a lawyer.
- **Center for Social Media at American University: Best Practices in Fair Use** http://www.centerforsocialmedia.org/fairuse.htm "Documentary filmmakers have created, through their professional associations, a clear, easy to understand statement of fair and reasonable approaches to fair use."
- **Chart on Rights Clearance Problems and Possible Solutions** http://www.law.duke.edu/cspd/pdf/docfilmchart.pdf
- **Copyright Overview** http://www.law.cornell.edu/wex/index.php/Copyright
- **The Copyright Act: 17 U.S.C. §§ 101-1332** http://www.law.cornell.edu/uscode/html/uscode17/usc_sup_01_17.html
- **Copyright and Fair Use** http://fairuse.stanford.edu
- **Copyright Term and the Public Domain** http://www.copyright.cornell.edu/training/Hirtle_Public_Domain.htm
- **United States Copyright Office** http://www.copyright.gov

Selected Organizations
- **Center for the Study of the Public Domain** http://www.law.duke.edu/cspd
  The home of the Arts Project that brought you this comic.
- **Center for Social Media** http://www.centerforsocialmedia.org
  The home of the Best Practices Statement.

- **Chilling Effects Clearinghouse** http://www.chillingeffects.org
Chilling Effects aims to help Internet users understand the protections that the First Amendment and intellectual property laws give to online activities, with a particular focus on cease and desist letters.
- **Creative Commons** http://creativecommons.org
Creative Commons builds upon the "all rights reserved" of traditional copyright to create a voluntary "some rights reserved" copyright. It is a nonprofit and all of the tools are free.
- **Electronic Frontier Foundation** http://www.eff.org
The premier online civil liberties organization.
- **Full Frame Documentary Film Festival** http://www.fullframefest.org/main.html
The leading documentary film festival in the United States. Takes place each spring in Durham, North Carolina.
- **Motion Picture Association of America** http://www.mpaa.org
Founded in 1922, the MPAA is the trade association of the American film, video and television industry.
- **Public Knowledge** http://www.publicknowledge.org
Representing the public interest in intellectual property policy.
- **Volunteer Lawyers for the Arts** http://www.vlany.org
VLA provides *pro bono* legal services, and educational programs, to the arts community in New York and beyond.

ACKNOWLEDGMENTS

Bound By Law grew out of a conference on the effects of intellectual property law on music and film, which was held in conjunction with the Full Frame Documentary Film Festival. Both the conference and the production and distribution of this book were made possible by a grant from the Rockefeller Foundation. Other support was also provided by the Center for the Study of the Public Domain and by the Office of the President, Duke University.
Debts of gratitude are owed to many people: At Duke, to Garrett Levin, David Lange, Richard Riddell, Eileen Wojciechowski, Jordi Weinstock, Wayne Miller, Nick Drury, Jennifer Carpenter, Scott Lenger and Hiroki Nishiyama. In the filmmaking community Chris Hegedus, Orlando Bagwell and Davis Guggenheim gave us vital material while John Sloss offered a unique legal perspective.   Laurie Racine and Joan Shigekawa offered vital support. Peter Jaszi and Pat Aufderheide's work on fair use was invaluable. Larry Lessig's work provided the impetus to focus on documentary film and his scholarship is a vital resource in outlining problems in the area. Along the way, others supplied key encouragement or advice. Thanks to Cory Doctorow, Sham B., Brandt Goldstein, Megan Taylor, the people at Full Frame, and everyone else who made this project possible. Mona Aoki deserves special mention for patience verging on the saintly.